Fashion
Bites

Fashion Bites

Illustrations by Vic Riches

hardie grant books
MELBOURNE · LONDON

"Most of the *Vogue* girls are so thin, **tremendously thin,** because Miss Anna don't like fat people."

ANDRÉ LEON TALLEY,
contributing editor of American *Vogue*,
tells it like it is

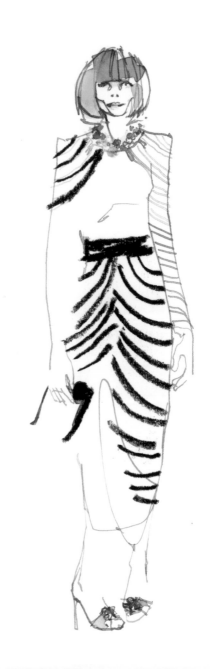

"Yes, some people say to me
'you're too skinny',
but never a skinny person says that to me,
only people who could
lose a few pounds say that."

KARL LAGERFELD:
once of ample girth,
now a fan of skinny jeans

"People have this idea that if they come into my store I'm going to make them walk out **with a seventeenth-century sailing ship on their head.**"

I wonder why,
PHILIP TREACY?

"I make **a lot** of money
and I'm worth
every
cent."

Humble

model

NAOMI CAMPBELL

"Nothing
tastes
as
good
as
skinny
feels."

Supermodel
KATE MOSS
has obviously
never eaten a
French pastry

"**I don't understand**
how a woman can leave the house
without fixing herself up a little –
if only out of politeness."

Wearing no make-up is the
height of rudeness
according to
COCO CHANEL

"No one wants to see curvy women.

You've got **fat mothers** with their bags of chips sitting in front of the television and **saying thin models are ugly.**

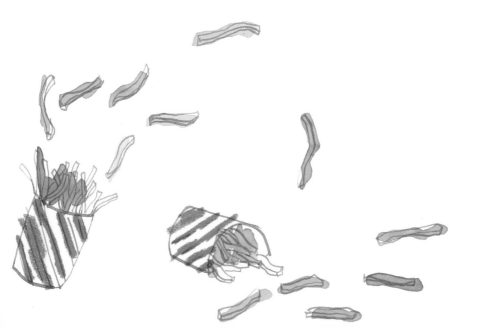

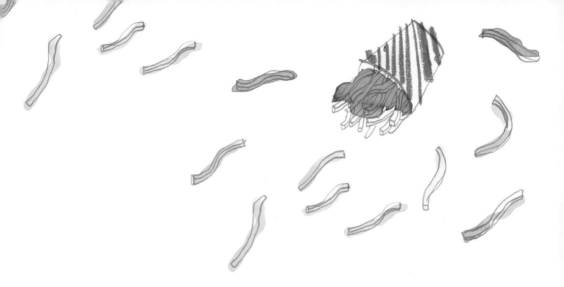

Fashion is about
dreams and illusions."

KARL LAGERFELD
doesn't want to see curves,
even if you do

"Never let your frog out-dress you."

Wise words
from blonde bombshell
MISS PIGGY

"An evening dress that reveals a woman's ankles while walking is the most disgusting thing I have ever seen."

Legendary Latin designer
VALENTINO
finds ankles
offensive

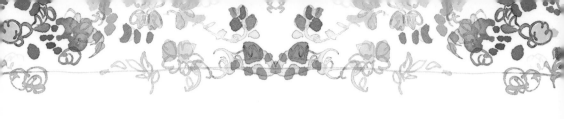

"I don't do fashion, I am fashion."

COCO CHANEL,
founder of Chanel and one of the
wittiest fashionistas
of all time

"The jean!

The jean is the destructor!

It is a dictator!

It is destroying creativity.

The jean
must be stopped!"

PIERRE CARDIN
disses denim

"You dress elegant women.

You dress sophisticated women.

I dress sluts."

The late, great

GIANNI VERSACE

calls a spade a ... slut

" There are no ugly women, only lazy ones. "

A back-handed compliment

from make-up guru

HELENA RUBINSTEIN

"People who move in [fashion] circles never have anything to say.

You know it's hard enough doing this job,
I don't have to fucking
live it as well.

I'd rather sit at home watching
Coronation Street."

ALEXANDER MCQUEEN
had a soft spot for the
Rovers Return

"Art produces ugly things which frequently **become more beautiful with time.**

Fashion, on the other hand, produces
beautiful things
which always become
ugly with time.

Profound words
from French Poet
JEAN COCTEAU

"When I think my hair needs a bit of help, I just glue another bit on to my head."

Eccentric fashionista
DAPHNE GUINNESS
explains her
Madame de
Pompadour
bouffant

"A woman who doesn't wear perfume has no future."

COCO CHANEL:
designer, psychic,
scent-lover

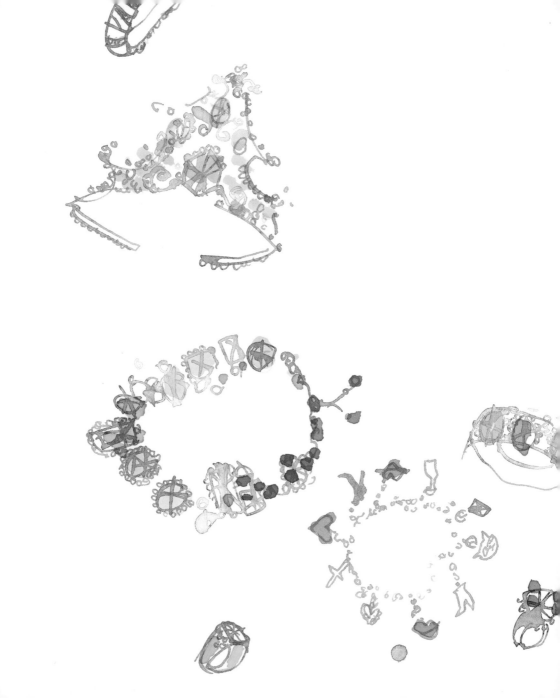

"The Milanese have made **bad choices,**
bad fashion,
and bad jewellery."

CHRISTIAN LACROIX:
pot, meet kettle?

"You can't cry because we don't have time to fix your make-up."

Make-up artist
JAY MANUEL
suggests you
suck it up

"All the American women had purple noses and gray lips and their faces were chalk white from terrible powder.

I recognized that the United States could be my life's work."

Thank goodness cosmetics queen

HELENA RUBINSTEIN

saved American women from
looking like The Joker

"A woman has
the age
she deserves."

COCO CHANEL
hadn't heard of
Botox
in her day

"Do you prefer
'fashion victim'
or
'ensembly challenged'?"

ALICIA SILVERSTONE
as Cher in *Clueless* had a
way with words

"Tom Ford once told me that he found French women sexier than American ones.

He said:

Americans are too clean...

I took no offence."

American fashion editor

LINDA WELLS:

unsexy but hygienic

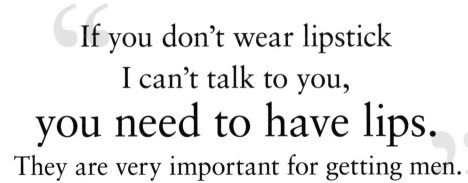

"If you don't wear lipstick
I can't talk to you,
you need to have lips.
They are very important for getting men."

The late
fashion icon
and red-lipstick enthusiast,
ISABELLA BLOW

"When Lagerfeld took over
the Chanel collections,

they had one foot in the
grave and the other

Former editor of *Women's Wear Daily*
and author of *Glue Gun Décor*
MARIAN MCEVOY

on a banana peel.

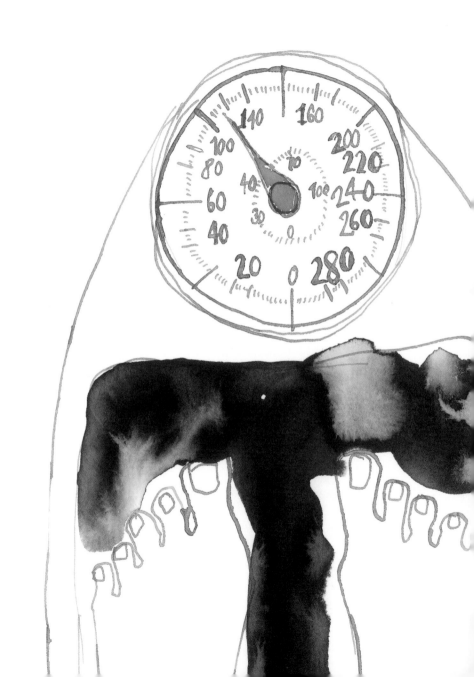

"Do me a favour and lose five pounds **immediately** or get out of my building, **like, now!**"

Inventor of the
piano-key necktie,
fashion mogul
MUGATU,
of comedy *Zoolander*

"I think people look awful these days, **and it depresses me.**

You see a production
of Hamlet and he's in a
bloody sweatshirt

or Polonius is in a
flipping tracksuit."

DAME VIVIENNE WESTWOOD,
on declining
sartorial standards

"To be honoured for the clothes I have worn is a special treat,

since I had to get dressed anyway."

Sometimes editor
of French *Vogue*,
sassy diva
MISS PIGGY

"Exercise exists for everyone, and you might try it before you get a suit."

Designer
HEDI SLIMANE
gives the
skinny
on suits

"The idea of making my own perfume makes me want to vomit."

Actress

EMMA WATSON

does not want to make a scent,

apparently

"I don't get out of **bed**
for less than
$10,000 a day."

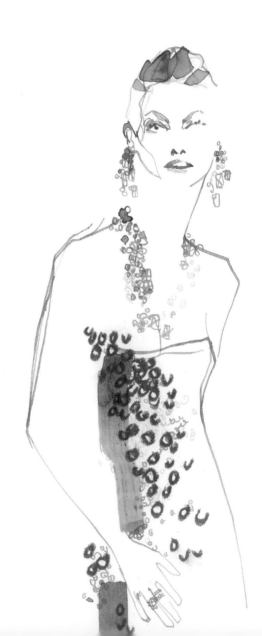

Well-rested
supermodel
LINDA EVANGELISTA

"I thought *Sex and the City* was supposed to be about cutting-edge fashion –

there was nothing remotely memorable or interesting about what I saw.

I went to the premiere and left after 10 minutes."

VIVIENNE WESTWOOD
may ask Carrie for the
wedding dress back

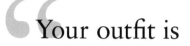"Your outfit is

more tragic

than magic."

Ex-model

IMAN

likes to rhyme

her snipes

"**Girl,** don't blame the photographer...

blame your parents for bad **DNA.**"

America's Next Top Model judge

J. ALEXANDER

believes the camera

never lies

"I'm not that interested in fashion...

When someone says that lime green
is the new black for this season,

you just want to tell them to

get a life."

British designer
BRUCE OLDFIELD
does not
suffer fools

"There is
no fashion
for the old."

Unfortunately for
COCO CHANEL
she lived until age 87

"Your collection is shabby chic. **Without the chic.**"

Who knew model

IMAN

was so

catty?

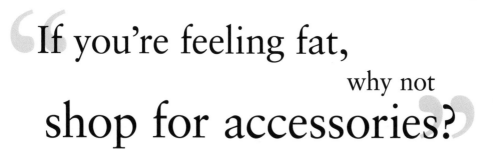

"If you're feeling fat, why not shop for accessories?"

Sage advice
from designer
LULU GUINNESS

"Never in the history of fashion

has **SO** little material

been raised **SO** high

to reveal **SO** much

that needs to be covered
SO badly."

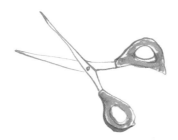

Fashion photographer

CECIL BEATON

was concerned about hemlines

"Do you know that cats can't wear corsets?

They can't stand!

Not at all!

They just fall over.

I know because I tried!"

JEAN PAUL GAULTIER'S

cat may be looking for

a new owner

Italian designer
ELSA SCHIAPARELLI
tells us what
we already know

"Women dress alike all over the world:

they dress to be

annoying to other women."

"You wanted to be on a yacht in the
south of France,

but you went
overboard.

IMAN is
nautical
but not
nice

"There are a lot of gay people in fashion,

but it's not as if **every gay person** is a **great creator.**"

CALVIN KLEIN

orders a
saucer of milk

"Anna and I, we've known each other **a long time.**

We have a real **mutual respect** for each other,

even though sometimes **I feel like killing her.**"

GRACE CODDINGTON,
creative director of American *Vogue*,
sometimes sees red

"I wish her all the luck in the world, just so long as

I don't have to see her anymore or hear her spoken about."

KARL LAGERFELD
on Ines de la Fressange, his EX-muse, who is clearly
not on his Christmas card list

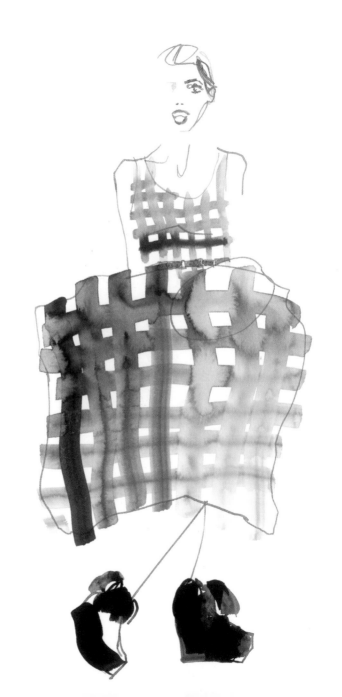

"Fashion is what you adopt when you don't know who you are."

English writer and raconteur
QUENTIN CRISP
could not abide a follower

"Enough of sweetness,

women need to get out there

and fight again."

MIUCCIA PRADA
has had
enough

"If you are not in fashion, you are nobody."

LORD CHESTERFIELD,
keeping it real
in the eighteenth century

" Fashion is a
form of ugliness so
intolerable
that we have to
alter it every six
months. "

OSCAR WILDE
hits the nail
on the head

"My friends, there are no friends."

A lonely
COCO CHANEL
never worked out she was
offending everyone

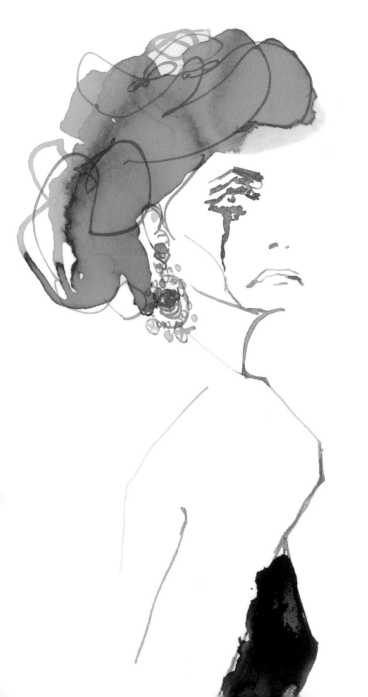

"She's a full-on Monet...
From far away, it's OK,
but up close,
it's a big old mess."

CHER in
Clueless reminds us of the
importance of art history

"I'm sure you have **plenty more poly-blend** where that came from.

NIGEL in *The Devil Wears Prada*:
more nasty than nice

"You either know fashion or you don't."

American *Vogue*
editor-in-chief
ANNA WINTOUR,
like her bob,
is blunt

Published in 2011 by Hardie Grant Books

Hardie Grant Books (UK)
Dudley House, North Suite
34–35 Southampton Street
London WC2E 7HF
www.hardiegrant.co.uk

Hardie Grant Books (Australia)
85 High Street, Prahran, Victoria, Australia 3181
www.hardiegrant.com.au

British Library Cataloguing-in-Publication Data. A catalogue record
for this book is available from the British Library.

ISBN 978-1-74270-176-9

Designer Joanna Byrne

Printed and bound in China by 1010

10 9 8 7 6 5 4 3 2 1

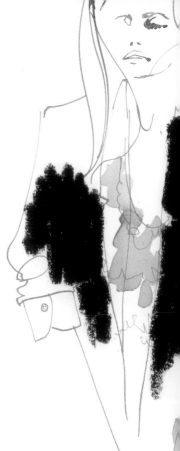

Vic Riches

Vic Riches was born in 1990 in London,
but grew up in Saffron Walden, Essex.
Her first published illustrations were done
when she was four, and she hasn't changed
her style since. Between designing clothes for
her Fashion Degree at Kingston University,
Vic can be found wandering around the
streets of London with a sketchbook.

vicriches.blogspot.com